GW00633544

FAST SEX

GREAT SEX
ANYTIME!
ANYWHERE!

Nicci Talbot

hamlyn

An Hachette Livre UK Company
www.hachettelivre.co.uk

First published in Great Britain in 2009 by
Hamlyn, a division of Octopus Publishing Group Ltd
2–4 Heron Quays, London E14 4JP
www.octopusbooks.co.uk
www.octopusbooksusa.com

Copyright © Octopus Publishing Group Ltd 2009

Distributed in the U.S. and Canada by
Octopus Books USA:
c/o Hachette Book Group USA
237 Park Avenue
New York NY 10017

All rights reserved. No part of this work may be
reproduced or utilized in any form or by any means,
electronic or mechanical, including photocopying,
recording or by any information storage and retrieval
system, without the prior written permission of
the publisher.

Nicci Talbot asserts the moral right to be identified
as the author of this work

ISBN 978-0-600-61781-5

A CIP catalogue record for this book is available
from the British Library

Printed and bound in Hong Kong

10 9 8 7 6 5 4 3 2 1

Warning
With the prevalence of AIDS and other sexually
transmitted diseases, if you do not practise safe sex
you are risking your life and that of your partner.

In many countries sex in a public place is illegal.

Contents

Introduction

The key to a happy sex life is maintaining a spirit of adventure and fun – the essence of the quickie. If you're in a long-term relationship you will probably have experienced the three stages of love, as recognized by sex researcher Dr Helen Fisher: from the first throes of lust and passion through the bonding of romantic love to the comfort of coupledom and possibly parenthood. The intensity of your sex lives may have dulled and become a little routine. This is where this guide to the art of fast, exciting sex will help you to keep things hot in the bedroom – and beyond.

A sexy little gift

Think of a quickie as an instant, intimate exchange with your lover – a daily reminder that you're still a couple in love and lust and that you appreciate each other as sexual beings. Do that and you open up a whole new language of sex.

One of the best descriptions of the quickie I've come across is a 'sexy little gift' to each other, which sums it up perfectly. As you'll discover, a quickie doesn't have to mean full sex, it is about making the most of opportunities to express your sexuality and desire, and this can be just as much fun on your own as well as with your partner.

By taking sex out of the bedroom the world is literally your playground. Having sex in unconventional places – at home, at work, at play – will give you a thrill that will intensify the pleasure of close encounters. These are fun, breathless sexual moments that most of us *would love* to be having more of – the tips and ideas included here are just a beginning.

The WORLD is your playground

Why quickies are good

Enjoying your body, and that of your lover, has many benefits, and a healthy sex life will do wonders for you physically and spiritually – quickies are a great way of relaxing as sex releases feel-good hormones. Quick sex is like a quick fix – the more sex you have, the more you want. Your libido will be revved up and you'll soon be looking for opportunities to let off some steam, whenever and wherever you happen to be. Being spontaneous and imaginative will give your relationship a new lease of life – sex will never be routine again.

I'm not suggesting that you should have quick sex all of the time. As psychologist Janice Hiller points out, it won't fix a relationship that's broken but it will pep up your sex life if you're in a good one. Quickies help you to live in the moment and to let go of adult responsibilities.

A note on timing

Choose your moments for a quickie. It's probably not a good idea to launch into your sexy striptease while he's watching his team on the TV, or to pounce on her when she's just walked in after a bad day. Communication and being aware of each other's needs is key to an enjoyable quickie. If your lover rejects your advances don't take it personally or give up trying to be spontaneous. Work out how you can resolve the problem for next time.

Daily *quickies* are good for your *mind, body and soul*

There are three types of quickie, according to sex coach Dr Tara Few, and the ideas offered within this book fall into the first two categories, hopefully eliminating any experience of the third.

The spontaneous quickie

Animalistic and wanton, this is the type of encounter that takes us by surprise. You feel a sudden urge to have sex – *right now*. It's exciting, fun and a huge risk if you're in a public place. It signifies passion and spontaneity and makes you feel alive.

The planned quickie

Planned encounters require a little forethought and organization – with busy lives, careers and children the opportunities for impulsive sex are limited. If we want to maintain momentum, fun and excitement in our sex lives we need some forward thinking. Send your lover a sexy text or a dirty email to create anticipation, build excitement and get your adrenaline flowing – ensuring your sex life and relationship stay fun and fresh.

The lazy quickie

Sex when you're tired and can't be bothered or you're preoccupied and not in the mood, isn't good sex but you do it anyway out of habit or because you feel guilty. We've all done this. There may be a time and a place for it but if it becomes a regular habit you're in trouble. This kind of sex is not in the true spirit of the fulfilling quickie.

The right type
of quickie

Acting on impulse

What does a quickie mean to you?

Before you embark on the fast sex train, it's worth taking a moment to ask yourself what a 'quickie' means to you, and your partner: define what you'd like and where you'd like it and open your mind to being sensual and sexual, not always taking things to their climactic conclusion.

I did a quick poll to find out how we define the quickie and the results are revealing. It's not necessarily about full sex and orgasm as that's not always practical; if you're trying to achieve this it can add stress and expectation to something that's supposed to be light-hearted and fun. It's the quality of the quickie that counts – feeling desired and wanted is the key to a successful quickie and happy relationship.

Quickies can be:
• a deep kiss
• caressing the back of your neck
• oral sex
• a foot rub when you've just got home
• a dirty whisper in public
• a sexy text
• prolonged eye contact
• a neck and shoulder rub
• playing with yourself at your desk
• washing your lover's hair
• massaging his cock as he leaves for work.

Aim for a range of sexual experiences in your relationship and make time for sensuality so that when the opportunity for a quickie comes along you really enjoy it.

A quickie is a great way to keep you feeling connected

Do what comes **naturally to you** and get into the habit of giving yourself regular 'quickies' throughout the day, whether that's **thinking about sex** or playing with yourself – your body will be tuned in and sensitive to touch

Basic instincts

Basic instincts

Myth:
Men love *quickies* and women prefer to take their time over love-making

Not true! Women love quickies just as much as men do and their bodies and brains are hot-wired to get aroused as quickly as men. There's a lot written about how quickly a man can come, and how long a woman can take, but our natural instincts are to be turned on, primed and ready for intercourse within seconds.

The evolutionary theory about fast sex is that once upon a time women needed to be able to respond instantly to the stranger who rode into town – to get wet quick (within 10–15 seconds), have sex and so extend the gene pool. Men are also biologically programmed to become aroused quickly for similar reasons.

Although intercourse within seconds may not be particularly satisfying, you can make the most of your basic instincts to enjoy being turned on; kissing, playing with each other, and with sex toys, to heighten the tension and pleasure. This type of sex is as much a part of a woman's sexual fantasy as a man's – think of it as sexual equality – and is the reason why fast sex is still an urge we can't resist.

Forbidden fruits

Illicit sex is exciting – doing something you shouldn't where you shouldn't is thrilling, and is why the location for fast sex is almost as important as what you're doing. The anticipation of discovery, the possibility of being seen and watched, the urgency of time all add up to a heady mix of pleasure. We often associate affair sex with quickies because they're all about limited time and not getting caught. The possibility that you might get caught can be an aphrodisiac, says psychologist Janice Hiller.

Affairs are exciting but it's not necessarily the risk that excites us, more that we're in a focused situation. There's no intrusion, no domestic worries to deal with so the situation is intensified. Our brains are already aroused before we start to touch and this feels electric.

I'm not suggesting that you go off and have an affair to experience hot sex, just that you take the principles behind it and apply them to your own relationship. We all need a few hours in a different setting, away from the realms of domesticity.

Fast sex facts

Location is a key element in exciting sex and the facts prove that we're making the most of any opportunities that come our way. According to a survey carried out by Mates Healthcare:

- 40 per cent of us have had sex in the garden
- over two-thirds of us have had sex in a car
- 45 per cent of us have had sex in a field
- 41 per cent have had sex on a beach
- 94 per cent of us think outdoor sex is a good way to keep a relationship healthy and happy.

The **thrill** comes from getting away from the familiar, in **doing new things together** and having adventures

Quickie quotes

This is how a few quickie followers have described their experiences:

'A quickie offers an escape from the day-to-day humdrum, *a flavour of excitement* and our free selves not chained down to endless chores – able to feel pleasure even when we're not in the moment to. I love it when I am all stressed out and on my way to a busy event and my partner briefly massages my pussy or plays with his cock for me. It gives me a brief taste of things to come and look forward to and reminds me of *what is truly important* – our love and giving each other pleasure.'

'We had a quickie *on the bonnet* of our car once. We'd had bit to drink and I remember seeing a *security camera* nearby. "Who cares?", we thought. If they object they'll make it known. It was great fun – I think the alcohol definitely helped!'

'On the roof of a bus station. Oh, and in a dinghy. I'm a hedonist. I think *you should try everything once, then twice*, just in case you didn't get it right the first time, and three times, to be really sure...'

'It's important to go off for the day and have an adventure – just the two of you. *Be creative and spontaneous* in daily life. I once slipped a pocket vibrator into my coat pocket when we were going out. I'd not used it for ages so I thought, *why not?*'

'If I'm meeting my partner for lunch, I like to spend the morning *texting and chatting online* to help my mind and body prepare for sex. By the time we meet for 40 minutes or so I'm completely wet and desperate for sex.'

'We were having **an affair** and so the idea of secret meetings and getting caught, snatches of time here and there, was thrilling. **A huge turn on.**'

'I think we get **too hung up on orgasms** sometimes. Why not just enjoy a quickie as a way of being intimate with one another? It takes ages to come sometimes so if we only thought about sex as a means to orgasm we'd never do it! I think **it takes the pressure off** if we let go of the whole orgasm idea.'

'**Playful and fun.** Pulling my jeans down in the kitchen when I'm cooking or washing up without undoing the buttons first. Usually when we've got company in the lounge. I pretend to be annoyed but **he knows I love it.** Or when he puts his hands inside my shirt to rub my nipples when I'm on the laptop.'

'*Location, location, location.*'

Warming up

Make time for sex. Cut back on time spent in front of the TV and capitalize on the times you're together. By scheduling a quickie into your diaries you'll both be feeling hot and ready when your plan comes together.

With your lover, start by making a list of the type of sex you'd like to be having and where. Write dates in the diary. If necessary, plan childcare in advance so you have intimate time to yourselves.

Perfect plans

Write down 10 ideas for hot quickies, ask your lover to do the same and put them into a box or hat. Set aside 10 minutes that you can devote to each other. Take it in turns to pull one idea out of the box and for the next 10 minutes you have to fulfil the chosen desire – perhaps a foot rub or back massage, for starters.

Give **sex** as much *priority* as you do other things in your life

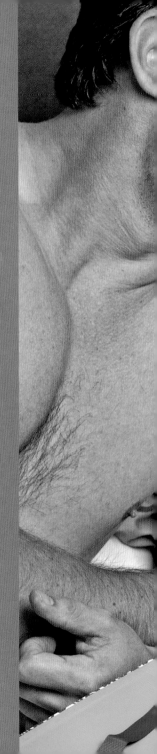

Try a **lucky** dip

Box of delights

There are plenty of special treats to help get you in the mood, quick. It's worth investing in a toy box to keep close at hand. Stock it with lubes (silicone-based for the shower, flavoured for oral sex) and massage oils, and a range of vibrators, such as pocket-sized bullets, remote control ones you can wear out-and-about to tease each other, and a finger vibe or a cock ring to use on him for a fast turn on.

Shopping for your toy box is a quickie in itself. Try on a strap-on in the changing rooms or test out the intensity of a vibrator on your hand. Take it in turns to buy something new for your sex life each week.

Experiment with oils and herbs that increase and quicken arousal, such as Zestra, a female arousal gel, or supplements like Libidofemme and LibidoForte, to heighten sensation, lubrication and increase sex drive.

Play with your *toys* nicely

Retail sex therapy

Sex and shopping – can it get much better? Turn the weekly shop into an erotic adventure and stock up with all things aphrodisiac so that you can throw together a sexy supper in minutes. Make sure there is plenty of finger food to feed to each other. Sucking the butter off an asparagus spear or sharing a juicy strawberry are great ways of enjoying a brief, sensual moment.

Passionate, greedy sex calls for energy so ensure you're both getting enough libido-boosting nutrients from whole foods, fish oils and foods high in zinc.

Seek out perfume shops (some have wind-machines that blow in your face to turn you on and seduce you into buying) and find a scent that sets your pulse racing – those with vanilla or almond are tried and tested. Go to a bakery and indulge in a fresh warm loaf, or cinnamon-topped bagel (cinnamon is an aphrodisiac for men).

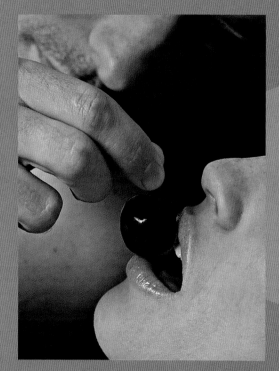

Discover the *hidden pleasures* on the high street

Dressing the part

What you're wearing, or not, can play a huge part in setting the mood and is as much a part of quickie sex as when you get it together. Why not go panty-less? It's a great tease and makes for easy access. Adopt a sexy style of dress – heels will change your mood, the way you walk and how your body moves. Taking care of your appearance, including a daily grooming and beauty regime, will make you feel good about yourself so that you exude confidence.

Choose your underwear carefully; hold-ups or the full suspender and stockings combo will make you feel hot, and the odd flash of lace and flesh will arouse his curiosity. Stripping is a classic tease, but try making him watch you dress or allowing him to lace up your corset or fasten your bra – it's intimate and sexy.

For a spontaneous quickie, rub your pussy juices into your neck and cleavage before asking him to help you dress – the scent is a natural pheromone and he won't know what's hit him.

Be a sex slave to your wardrobe

Girls, don't be shy! Masturbation helps you to stay connected to your sexual self. It's good for your skin, hair, PMT, and libido. It can help you to orgasm in a couple of minutes — ideal when you need some fast relief. Exploring your body helps you to find out what you like, makes you a more assertive and confident lover and enables you to share your discoveries with your partner. Being able to give yourself an orgasm alone is also very empowering.

Please yourself

Explore *your* own body

Clue up on your clit

Your clitoris is the size of a small pea and is at the top of the vulva, near the inner labia. A hood covers it, and three-quarters of it is underneath the skin, which is why general stimulation in the area feels good. When aroused, the clitoris becomes erect and you can see it properly. Prop yourself up with pillows on the bed and gently pull back the clitoral hood, so you get a good view.

Clitoral massage

Using a lubricant, massage all around the clitoris to warm it up. Use the palm of your hand as well as the tips of your fingers. Move your hand up and down, then across it and in circles to find out what feels good. Then gently flick and pull it, as it swells and becomes erect. When you find a stroke you like keep up a consistent rhythm and pressure until you orgasm.

G-spot massage

Once you're turned on you can try G-spot massage. Squat or kneel down and insert your first and middle fingers into the vagina with your palm facing upwards. Press firmly on the front wall, curving your fingers back in a 'come hither' motion. The G-spot feels spongy and raised and because it's close to the urethra, stroking it can make you want to pee. Gentle stroking feels good. You may feel blood rushing to your face after a few minutes and if this happens, keep going. Some women experience full body orgasms this way.

A-spot massage

The A-spot (anterior fornix zone) is a bit higher than your G-spot, on the front wall of the vagina below the cervix. Gentle stimulation here has been found to increase lubrication and sensation. Once you've identified your G-spot continue up a little higher along the front wall until you find an

Discover
girl power

Kiss me quick

Communicate your desires with more than words

A lingering glance or the brush of lips against skin will soon get you hot. Create little rituals that signify you want sex – *now* – like slipping into a pair of high heels or unbuttoning your shirt. Watch each other closely when you're having sex and during orgasm itself, then you'll be able to recall this intimate bond the next time you gaze into each other's eyes.

Kiss more – it's the ultimate quickie. Kiss her in the way you'd like to have sex with her – for many women kissing is the quickest turn on. The ancient Chinese believed that there's a link between the upper lip and the clitoris and the lower lip and the penis. It explains why there's an instant throb between your legs whenever your lips meet.

Tell your lover what you'd like to do to them and how sexy you find them, then use this erotic language to turn each other on – especially hot if you're in a public place. Repeating a few trigger words that you normally use during sex will instantly transport you and your lover to that highly-charged scenario.

Discovering desire

It's easy to lose the connection with your sexual nature in the daily grind. But you can rediscover your sexual energy through simple things, like going for an energetic walk, dancing the tango or simply finding time to relax and focus on yourself and your desires. Ask yourself about the type of sex that appeals to you. Do you initiate sex? Do you recognize your own sexual desire?

Keep a sex diary. Note down all your random dreams, thoughts and fantasies; things that have turned you on today and times that you want sex. Are you a morning person or do you prefer to cosy up together in the evening? Work out your sexiest time of day so that you can make the most of it.

Your hormones control your sex drive – a woman's sex drive is believed to peak during ovulation. Men have a daily cycle with testosterone peaking early morning, which is why he's usually horny first thing. However, it's thought that 3pm is a woman's sexiest time of day, so factor in a late lunch or two to take advantage!

Watching porn, together or independently, is a fast track way to feeling hot and ready. Studies have shown that the visual and erotic circuits in the male brain are closely connected, so his arousal can be fast – he can ejaculate and orgasm within a few minutes of stimulation. Although a woman needs a bit more time to get really horny, she is still quick to respond to visual stimulation – studies have shown that women are even capable of having an orgasm via imagery alone.

Triple X pleasures

If porn gives you a warm flush and sets your heart racing, you're well on your way to a great quickie. Build on this sensation by thinking about sex during the day; fantasize; notice the sensual around you; imagine yourself in a sexy scenario wherever you are; share an erotic story and look at erotic images. Visualizing a quickie the way you'd like it to happen before you get together gives your body a head start and gets your juices flowing in anticipation.

Watching porn can be enough for you to climax without touching yourself

Enjoy some visual stimulation

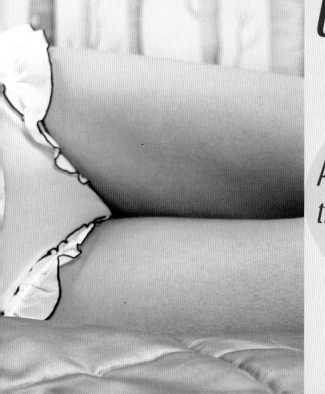

Feeling loved, appreciated and desired fuels our sex drive, so when you're apart let each other know how you feel and what you want to do when you meet. Leave little notes in her handbag or his suit jacket to make your lover laugh, feel good and ensure they're thinking about you all day.

Keeping yourself sexually charged throughout the day is simply a case of reminding yourself of your desires once in a while – send a dirty text or leave a voicemail message to let your lover know how hot you are.

Experiment with body jewellery. A long necklace that tickles your nipples and clitoris will ensure you're kept on the edge. Cock jewellery will tug on his genitals when he walks, giving him little rushes of pleasure. Some items can be worn as normal jewellery as well as genital jewellery, which is both erotic and suggestive as you can use it to subtly communicate your desires to your lover.

Charged up

Absence makes the heart grow fonder

Kiss me quick

Kissing is a great way to communicate your desires. No two share the same style or characteristic. Are you in the mood for a passionate quickie? Tell him with a firm kiss. Lips remind us of genitals hence the pleasure he feels when he sees your soft, red lips. In erotica, there's a link between a woman's upper lip and her clitoris and a man's lower lip and his genitals so a gentle nibble here will turn you both on.

Warming up

Stand in front of your lover and as you come close tilt your head in the opposite direction to his. Relax your facial muscles and keep your lips soft and open as they gently meet. Use your hands to caress his neck, face and hair – whatever comes naturally. Close your eyes and lose yourself totally in the kiss.

Kissing to
connect

Kissing to communicate

The soul kiss

This kiss was so-called by the French who believe that the soul can be passed through the breath and tongue from one person to another. Gently part your lover's lips and explore her tongue and mouth using the tip of your tongue, as it is highly sensitive. Tease her by sucking on her tongue gently and pressing it down. It's fun to do this using ice cubes made from champagne that you pass between each other's mouths.

The foot kiss

A highly erotic form of kissing if you're not too ticklish. It is the ultimate quickie after a long day on your feet. Wash your lover's feet first in a bowl of scented water and then gently suck his toes one by one, paying attention to the sensitive bits in between. Massage the balls of his feet and the ankles (some men find this highly erotic) before kissing his feet all over. This is a loving, intimate and pampering kiss.

Upside down kiss

This is a lovely way to reconnect if you're both doing different things around the house. You sit at the table and he comes up behind you, caressing your shoulders and neck before leaning in over the top of your head for a kiss. It sends shivers down your spine as you can feel his breath on your neck as you lean back to greet his mouth. He can make it extra sensual by kissing your eyelids first before working his way down to your mouth.

Domestic bliss

Home sweet home

It's convenient; you have lots of rooms to choose from with different surfaces and types of furniture to explore. There are locks on doors, which gives you some control, and best of all, if you're living together it allows for spontaneous quickies – transporting you instantly from the mundane to the erotic. It's the perfect place for trying new positions and having sex half-dressed. Soon you'll have filled your home with saucy memories, and you'll have had a great time preparing ways to have sex when you're out and about, too.

Take a tour around your house. Is it sensual and fit for a quickie? Is it warm enough? A warm house will make you want to strip off on the spur of the moment and wearing less makes you more aware of each other's bodies, too. Are there enough surfaces at the right height to get playful on? Is the lighting relaxing? Do you have erotic art that inspires and turns you on? Think about the decor and use colour to express your sexuality – red evokes passion. Music can make or break a mood – have some sexy compilations on your MP3 player to play around the house.

Your home is a great
playground for a quickie

We tend to associate sex with the bed, but fast, fun, exciting sex can be enjoyed using a whole range of furniture as your support. Some pieces are perfect for quickies – rocking chairs and over-sized armchairs are ideal, or indulge in some glamorous antique pieces for a sensual boudoir. Leather goes down a treat – it feels, smells and sounds sexy. Furnish each room with a 'useful' piece of furniture – a chair or stool in the bathroom will only add to the fun.

Are you sitting comfortably?

Armchair antics

Invest in a big mirror for your bedroom or lounge – watching yourself masturbate or having sex standing in front of a mirror is a huge turn on as well as a good opportunity for you both to see your own orgasm faces. It is also worth moving the furniture around every once in a while to change your perspective – and the view.

If you've exhausted the household furniture possibilities, explore the world of erotic furniture designed to be supportive enough for sex. You can buy stools to sit on with a hole in the middle that enables your lover to give you oral sex while you're sitting above him.

Getting *up close* and *personal*

Cupboard love

The hall or cloakroom are transitory spaces in a house, but where better to snatch an impulsive quickie when you're overcome by passion? Simply push your lover against the wall, unbelt his trousers and give him an unexpected blow job, or bend her over the hall table with her skirt up around her waist ... if you get discovered use the excuse that you're just 'hanging up the coats'.

Small spaces are perfect for getting up close and personal. Cupboards or small cloakrooms feel a little bit kinky because they remind us of our childhood when we'd scuttle inside to hide after doing something we shouldn't. Enjoy your punishment for being naughty now. With little room for manoeuvre, your choice of positions is limited, but half the fun is finding a way to get inside her knickers. Standing sex against the wall feels wanton, and if she can sit on the sink or balance on the toilet seat, then you'll be able to get it together.

Many men rate blow jobs as their favourite sex act because they get to relax and surrender to the pleasure. A warm, wet mouth feels like a vagina and as the tongue is the strongest, most flexible muscle in the body it can bring him to climax very quickly. Use the tip of your tongue as well as the underside and base to vary the sensation and target his hot spots such as the frenulum and coronal ridge.

Oral sex for him

Face-sitting

If the mood is one of power play, try this submissive position. Get him to kneel over your face as you lie back on a pillow (he can use a special stool if it's more comfortable or if you feel he's going to squash you). Hold his cock at the base with your thumb and forefinger to control the speed and depth of his thrust. You can use your other hand to slap or pinch his buttocks or finger his anus lightly while you suck his cock. If it feels comfortable, lie on the edge of the bed and tip your head back a little to align him with your throat so that you can take him a little deeper.

The straddler

This position is great for clitoral and pelvic stimulation. Push him back onto the bed (he can rest on his elbows to watch). Straddle one of his thighs, positioning yourself so that your clitoris and pelvic area are being massaged as you move. Rub some of your pussy juice onto the tip of his cock and make small circles using the palm of your hand, first in one direction then the other. Then take the head into your mouth and gently suck, building up a rhythm and pace once he's aroused. Continue circling the head with the tip of your tongue and then take him fully into your mouth.

Stand and deliver

Standing positions are great for quickies because they feel impulsive. Take your man by surprise and lead him wherever you desire – outdoors, around the house, even in the office. Push him against the wall and kneel down between his legs holding his thighs for support. With a little practice, you will be able to unzip his trousers just using your teeth. Create a ring around the base of his cock with your thumb and forefinger so you can control his thrust. A long, slow lick from base to top along the underbelly will emphasize his length. Use the flat part of your tongue to circle the shaft. When you want him to come concentrate on the frenulum and coronal ridge (where the glans and shaft meet). Flick and circle it with the tip of your tongue to make his knees buckle.

Take him by surprise
Go down on his
hot spots

Stairway to heaven

Greet your lover at the door and lead him by the tie to the stairs... The stairs are a great location for an exciting and immediate 'welcome home' or goodbye quickie as they're usually near the door. Still half-dressed, you can hold onto the banister while he takes you from behind or get him to give you oral sex while you sit a couple of steps above him and he kneels down below you.

Steps are great for mismatched heights – use this to your advantage if your lover is taller than you by sitting on a higher step. If you need a little more room, make the most of a landing to lie down on or flip over so he's behind you. Rise to the challenge of a winding staircase – there'll be plenty of positions that you can try once you get started and don't forget the cupboard-under-the-stairs for a hidden quickie.

Taking it *a* step *at a time*

Sofa suppers

The sofa is the second most popular place for a quickie after the bedroom. Not surprising since it has a sofa and chairs (with arms at about waist height that are perfect for bending over), ideal for having sex on and still relatively comfortable! Experiment with erotic furniture or invest in a real fire. Place a big, soft rug in front of it that will just call out for writhing naked bodies.

The lounge is a room where you'll be relaxed but you can soon change the tempo – wriggle into his lap while he's watching TV and give him a lap dance or pull him forward in the armchair, kneel between his thighs and give him a quick blow job. She can sit on the floor between your legs while you massage her shoulders, but you don't stop there...

Have plenty of soft, plump cushions to hand – they'll make a great alternative to a bed as well as preventing carpet burns! Blankets and throws will disguise wandering hands and unbuttoned jeans when you're snuggled up on the sofa and you have company.

Liven things up
in the living room

Making the
net curtains
twitch

Steamy windows

If you like the idea of possibly being seen or watched during sex, then a window setting has lots of potential. Tempt him over by leaning against the window ledge provocatively (a short skirt and no knickers should do the trick), he can play with you from behind while in full view of the neighbours or flip you around as you rest on the windowsill. Giving her oral sex in this position combines the hedonistic pleasure of being on display with the thrill of your tongue play.

For a more comfortable session, a bay window seat, padded with plump cushions, can be put to good use – try it for solo quickies or mutual masturbation.

Long, gauzy curtains blowing in the summer breeze evoke a romantic setting for a bit of a show. If you are in the mood for putting on a performance and have patio doors or a balcony, entice your lover in from outside with a striptease, discarding your clothes and underwear as you go to leave a trail to the bed.

Many women love oral sex and it can lead to powerful orgasms. The tongue is our strongest muscle so it makes sense to utilize all of it. The underside feels smoother than the top, which is covered in tiny bumps. Use the flat part to warm your lover up from bottom to top and the tip to focus on the clitoris. A little sucking and humming while you work adds pleasurable vibrations too.

Oral sex for her

Let your tongue talk
in different ways

Side by side

Rather than sitting between your partner's legs, lie beside her so your head approaches from an angle. This position enables you to move your tongue sideways across her vulva rather than up and down (this is how many women masturbate and it feels extra pleasurable). Alternate between shallow and deep licks, flicking and concentric circling around the clitoris. As she gets more excited gently suck the clitoris between your lips, as this makes blood rush to the surface. Once you've found a stroke she likes, keep at it until she climaxes. If your mouth gets tired you can use your nose to nudge her clitoris too.

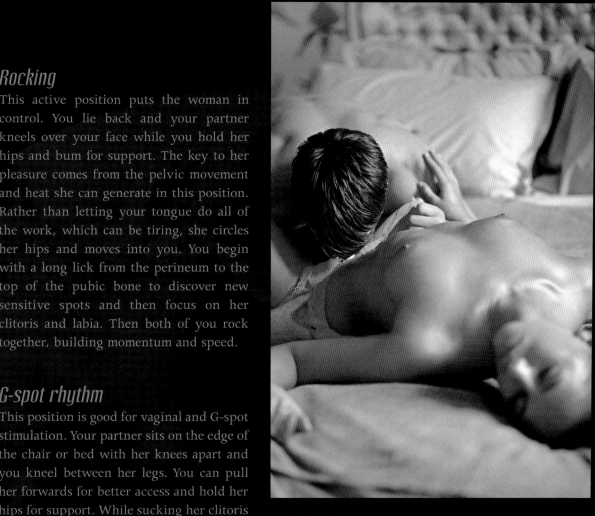

Rocking

This active position puts the woman in control. You lie back and your partner kneels over your face while you hold her hips and bum for support. The key to her pleasure comes from the pelvic movement and heat she can generate in this position. Rather than letting your tongue do all of the work, which can be tiring, she circles her hips and moves into you. You begin with a long lick from the perineum to the top of the pubic bone to discover new sensitive spots and then focus on her clitoris and labia. Then both of you rock together, building momentum and speed.

G-spot rhythm

This position is good for vaginal and G-spot stimulation. Your partner sits on the edge of the chair or bed with her knees apart and you kneel between her legs. You can pull her forwards for better access and hold her hips for support. While sucking her clitoris slowly insert two fingers into the vagina (palm facing upwards). The entrance to the vagina is the most sensitive part. Feel along her upper wall until you find her G-spot and then stroke it firmly while continuing to suck her clitoris using the same rhythm.

Kitchen sink dramas

Time to *turn up the heat*

The kitchen is great for dirty, impromptu quickies – it's usually warm and cosy with plenty of food to play with, easy floors to clean and work tops and tables to sit on.

Next time she's cooking or at the sink, sneak up from behind, slip your hands around her waist, kiss the back of her neck and play with her breasts until she's moaning with pleasure. Then lift her skirt and massage her pussy. You could just tease her and leave it there, or sit her on the edge of the kitchen work top with her legs wrapped tightly around your back while you slip inside. Next time she's back at the sink she'll have a secret smile on her face.

The kitchen table is often sturdy enough for a deep kiss and cuddle and if you're in the middle of eating then incorporate a few tasty morsels into the fun. Sex and food are a great combination and what better location for a blow job than up against the fridge?

Spice it up

Playing with your food

Playing Playing

Using food for its aphrodisiac effects has long been considered a sensual treat – stock up with sweet sauces and libido-boosting dips to smear and share. Fill the fruit bowl with phallic bananas, suggestive figs and delicious raspberries and strawberries – known as fruit nipples in erotica. Eating a fruit salad off each other's bodies will get all your juices flowing.

Cooking together can all be part of the fun (especially if you're both naked) – lick each other's fingers, taste-test small morsels then share the meal, feeding each other. A blindfold will add to the excitement and you could always set up a 'picnic' in front of the fire to tantalize much more than just your lover's taste buds.

63

Certain foods can boost your sex life: ginger and chilli stimulate blood flow to the genitals; avocados aid stamina; peanuts intensify orgasms and soft fruit will make his come taste that bit sweeter. Keep the bubbly on ice – he won't forget a champagne blow job in a hurry.

Fast spin

Fast spin Fast

The smell of fresh laundry can be a turn on, and sitting on the washing machine while it's on fast spin may be a bit of a cliché, but it's worth trying anything once. Go for the fastest spin and use a vibrator to tip you over the edge.

Overhead racks and clothing hooks can be hung on to while you're both standing or try a sturdy ironing board for support.

As for the pegs – use them for nipple play if you're so inclined.

Make everyday chores much more fun – grab the opportunity for a quick strip and sneak up on him from behind while he's emptying the washing machine. Slip your hands inside his trousers to pull them down, whispering 'I think you forgot these darling, they look like they need a wash...'

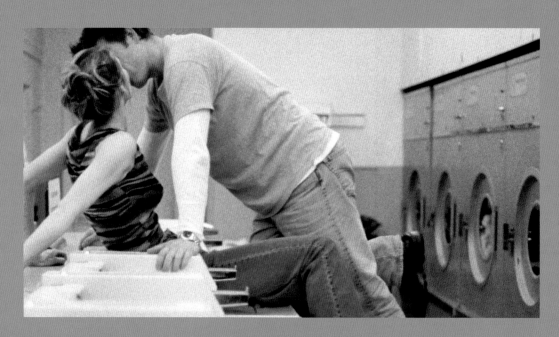

Hanging out the
dirty washing

Table manners

The dining room is often reserved for more formal occasions so getting it on here feels all the more illicit. For tabletop fun, make sure the table is sturdy enough for the both of you, or try the sideboard. Lie on the table naked (you or him) and dine Japanese-style, eating finger foods off your bodies using only your mouth.

Dining room chairs can be gripped and bent over for doggy-style sex or take up a seat at the head of the table with your legs over his shoulders as he tips you over the edge with his tongue.

If it's dinner for two use candles to create the right atmosphere. Soy candles have a cooler wax that you can drip on to each other's bodies from a height, or try edible candles – nibbling the wax off nipples or bare torsos. Some sex shops sell emollient massage candles made from natural wax and plant extracts – you can dribble them over the skin then let your hands glide and smoothe in the oils.

Private dining for two

Take it lying down

Sex surveys frequently put the Missionary at the top of women's position wish list, which is no surprise as it's highly intimate, enables kissing and full body and eye contact. Lying positions are comfortable and great for morning quickies (sleep naked for easier access) or for when you're cuddled up cosy on the sofa together.

Scissors

This position lets your man take the dominant position while you enjoy relinquishing control. Lie on your back with your legs apart, straight and extended upwards like a pair of scissors. He sits between your thighs and gently penetrates you, using his forearms to support himself. Flex your toes to tighten your grip so that it feels as if you are 'holding' him inside. Remain still while he enters you shallowly to begin with and then more deeply, alternating his pace. Squeeze your thighs and pelvic muscles together as he thrusts to build your orgasm. He can contract his PC (pubococcygeal) muscles too, to give you an extra shot of pleasure. This position works best on a firm mattress.

Who says the *missionary position* is boring?

A tight squeeze

This variant on the basic missionary position puts you in control, increasing sensation and fullness. Lie on your back and once he is inside you bring your legs together to hold him in place. This increases friction and a feeling of being filled up, which some women enjoy. Try contracting your pelvic muscles as he thrusts as this will double the intensity for both of you. You can also do this one lying on your stomach against a hard mattress, closing your legs after he's entered you.

The explorer

For deeper penetration try this variation. Position yourself at the edge of the bed. He kneels or stands in front and enters you holding on to your hips (use a cushion beneath your bum to lift you higher). Because your feet are touching the floor you can use them to move against him while he can explore different parts of your vagina, using your hips for leverage. You will be moving on and around his penis as he thrusts in and out, varying his speed and depth as he does so.

The desk job

There can be many advantages to working from home – finding time for a quickie is just one of them. A solo quickie is a great way to revive and refresh yourself. Take a play break for five minutes – keep a vibrator in the desk drawer and pop it into your knickers on slow to warm you up. Squeeze your pelvic muscles around it and when you're ready to come recline the chair and turn up the dial. A few naughty thoughts and a little porn on the laptop works a treat, too.

The boss/secretary fantasy is perfect for the home study – serve 'refreshments' when he's due a break: give him a neck massage to warm him up, then push the papers off the desk and sit in the middle of it while he stands in front of you. A sturdy desk and swivel chair (preferably leather) are essential – spin the chair around and straddle him so he's powerless to move. Take advantage of the distraction of a phone call to crawl beneath the desk and nudge her legs apart to give her oral sex.

Make use of modern technology to keep things interesting. Store some sexy pictures of yourself on your laptop or mobile to send to him during the day. If you've been keeping track of your horny days, add these to your calender and send him an online appointment to join you for a meeting in the office.

Taking a *play break*

A refreshing shower can take on a whole new meaning. A recent report discovered that shower massage is one of the most popular ways for women to orgasm – try it with a removable shower head to warm up your clitoris, making sure the water temperature and pressure are constant. You could invest in a double shower head for the ultimate in shower sex. Twice the water power pounding on your back feels very erotic – like your own private waterfall.

Wash your lover's hair in the shower for the ultimate sensual quickie as your scalp is full of nerve endings.

Act on impulse and take your lover by surprise by joining her fully dressed in the shower. It signals desire; you want her so badly that you couldn't wait to get undressed and slip inside.

To stop anyone slipping, use a non-slip mat and it's safest if she bends over while you're having sex.

Shower fresh

Getting all
lathered up

73

The bathroom is the perfect setting for a sensual encounter – you are warm, naked and wet and a locked door won't arouse suspicion. Take advantage to indulge in a quickie using the sink to sit on while you wrap your legs around your lover's back or flip around to hold on to it while he takes you from behind. Watching yourselves in a big mirror at the same time is a huge turn on.

Keep some waterproof sex toys to hand. The Brush Bunny is a tiny vibe that fits on the head of your electric toothbrush and there are some good waterproof toys for couples, such as a vibrating cock ring. You can hold the control box and monitor the vibrations, while he places the bullet end of the ring under his balls, or flips it around to hold against your clitoris.

Hide a small vibrator with your toiletries and a stash of naughty stories by the toilet and indulge in solo play sessions on a big, comfy chair in the corner.

A quick dip

The **bathroom** is
your best bet for quick,
uninterrupted play

Fresh and wild

Back to nature

Sex outdoors makes us feel alive, at one with nature and our bodies. Experiencing such physical pleasure in the fresh air and sunshine is one of the best feelings in the world – if you've tried it you'll know that nothing can beat it. It's about recapturing our youth, getting back to basics and enjoying ourselves as we're supposed to – as human beings feeling pleasure and a life without all the trappings. It's also practical if you don't have much intimate outdoor space at home.

Much of modern life is confined to small spaces – from home to car to desk and back again – and we're craving ways to break free from our roles and responsibilities and express ourselves. Outdoor quickies are one way to do this and if they suit your temperament and attitude to risk, then you'll thrive on them. While the thrills of being discovered add to the sexual tension, an outdoor quickie should be handled with care – act responsibly and never put yourself or your partner in a position that could be dangerous or illegal.

Remember to clean up after yourselves. There's nothing more unappealing than stumbling (or slipping) on a used condom in the park or woods. It's dangerous for children and animals, too. Enjoy your quickie responsibly!

Essential kit for the adventurous quickie:

- mobile phone
- bag for rubbish
- condoms
- lubricant (silicone-based lasts longer in the water)
- a big rug or blanket
- warm clothes (it will be much cooler in wooded, damp areas)
- sensible shoes (you may need to make a run for it!)
- torch
- towels for skinny-dipping
- bottle of water
- a change of outfit if you're heading somewhere afterwards.

Acting on your animal instincts

A garden with plenty of big bushes (evergreens are the best for privacy), overgrown grass, sturdy trees (for standing sex) and hidden spaces is great for getting down and dirty, and discovering a taste for sex in the outdoors. Your basic instincts will come in to play and you'll find plenty of inspiration for impromptu sex sessions, especially when the sun is shining.

Earthly delights

Lie back on a sunlounger or in a deckchair for a spot of oral sex, or try the thrills of setting the hammock rocking. Go panty-less and tease your lover with a flash of flesh by playing on the garden swing as he watches, he can then join you and nobody will be able to tell what you're up to if you wear a long skirt or sarong.

Keep a blanket or two handy in the shed or garage and if there's room add a comfy armchair – you can sneak off for a quickie if you've got visitors. With an outdoor heater you can enjoy sex under the stars.

Get more than *your* *fingers* *dirty*

Cars *are the ultimate* sex symbol

Cars represent speed, power and a fantastic sense of freedom. With a certain degree of privacy and relative comfort they're great for a spontaneous quickie – and you can make a fast getaway. Wait for a lay-by, service station, car wash or quiet spot before you park up and make your move – but watch out for security cameras.

With the seat tilted back you can give him a killer blow job, or slide into his lap with your knees up and feet away from the handbrake. A sunroof will give you a few more options as she can crouch in the front seat with her head out of the top keeping watch, while you give her oral sex. Having a vibrator, condoms and lube handy in the

From 0 to 60 in seconds

glove box will mean that you're ready for any impromptu pit-stops.

A little foreplay while driving will give off the right signals; try stroking her pussy or his cock when waiting for the lights to change. Even when travelling alone, you can use a hands-free phone to talk dirty to your lover.

Strip off
and take a back seat

Room with a view

Quickies on a balcony may require a little forward planning but that's all part of the excitement and anticipation, and if you're lucky enough to have a balcony at home, then don't overlook it when seeking out new venues for impromptu outdoor sex.

Book a hotel room and make sure it has a balcony. Hide behind the plants and use the railings to hold on to while your lover stands behind you. It's a good idea to suss out how overlooked you are and what risks you're willing to take. If all's clear hitch up her skirt for doggy-style sex – you get to enjoy two views!

If you'd rather not be in full view of your neighbours, use a chair or plant to shield you while you kneel down and give her oral sex on the balcony – it'll look like she's sunbathing. If you're feeling extra adventurous, venture outside your room and look for hidden corridors, a rooftop terrace or even a fire escape ...

Taking it on the **balcony**

The advantage of a hand job is that it can be done quickly and discreetly, even in public. Whereas fellatio requires privacy, hand jobs can be given beneath a table or under a long coat. Skin is our largest erogenous zone, so tease him elsewhere before moving down below. Make sure your hands are clean and your nails are filed. Find a comfortable angle and position and ask him to play with himself so you can see how he likes it.

Hand jobs for him

Give your man a helping hand

The back hander

This technique mimics how he masturbates so he'll find it super arousing. Kneel behind him on the bed or floor and reach around to stroke his inner thighs first. Then hold his cock at the base and slowly start to move up and down the shaft with both hands (use plenty of lube). Build up a smooth rhythm and keep your hands in contact with him at all times. When you reach the glans, cup your fist over it as if you're unscrewing a jar. This action will massage his frenulum and coronal ridge, both of which are highly sensitive. Use a string of pearls or a silk scarf as an erotic alternative to your hands.

Lacing

The underbelly of his penis is incredibly sensitive yet often ignored. Sit in front of him and gently push it back onto his belly so you can see it. Briefly massage any hot spots and trace along his veins. Bring his cock back and lace your fingers together, keeping them straight so that he's clasped between your fingers and thumbs. Start to move rhythmically up and down to build friction. Then curve your fingers over your hands and pump him a little faster from the base to the top.

Squeeze and hold

Try this technique first thing in the morning, as it will energize his whole body and set him up for the day. Sit beside him and hold his penis firmly at the base with one hand, forming a ring around it with your thumb and forefinger, gently pressing it down. Then squeeze and hold the shaft from bottom to top using your other hand. This form of genital massage will bring blood to the surface and help to strengthen his erection. Once he's hard you can make your movements more fluid if you want him to orgasm.

Beaches are the perfect playground

Sun, sea, sand... and sex

Warm sun on bare flesh, relaxation and anonymity all add to the thrills and heighten the senses when you're lying on the sand. Seek out remote coves and hideaways for more private spaces, or a nudist beach without families. Take a big rug to lie on, use towels and sarongs or umbrellas to create a little privacy, then have some fun. Spooning is a discreet position and while it may look like you're dozing, you can play and tease each other with ease.

An oily sunscreen will ensure you slip, slide and ride as well as protecting you from the rays – use it like massage oil, paying particular attention to those sensitive places like nipples; you wouldn't want them to get sunburnt, would you?

With the gentle caress of the water as it laps against your skin, a dip in the sea (naked or with just a bikini) is a sensual pleasure. While full sex isn't particularly easy or recommended in the salt water, your hands can explore beneath the surface. If you like the look and feel of rubber, then a wetsuit will serve any fetish fantasies.

Getting back to _nature_

Down in the woods

The countryside affords plenty of opportunities for exciting sex – woods, lakes, river banks, fields – all have thrill potential. Be prepared and look for remote spots with plenty of hiding places, avoiding popular beauty areas or dog walking routes and hiking trails – the last think you want is to be caught with your pants down by a group of ramblers.

Lakes are great for skinny-dipping, as are waterfalls. Once you're used to the temperature of the water it feels quite sexy to have it swirling around between your legs when you're naked. The cool water will set your skin tingling and you can always warm up together on the river bank beneath a large towel...

In a wood, lean her up against the tree facing you – that way you can both act as lookout in opposite directions, and keep the volume down, as noise can carry through the trees. Turn a run together through a woodland glade into a game of kiss chase; whoever catches the other first has to remove one item of clothing...

Folly frolics

You don't usually have to go too far to find an old ruin, folly, castle or barn that can play host to a fast-sex scenario. The idea of doing something completely inappropriate on ancient ground sends a tingle up the spine. There's a sense of being watched, of mystery and wondering who's been there before you and what naughty goings-on it has seen. Choose your timing carefully — there will be fewer visitors around in the early morning or midweek.

A quick hand or blow job can be enjoyed in the shadows of crumbling doorways, or use the tumbled ruins to hide behind for standing sex. Old fireplaces, steps and walls can all be used for support and a quickie in a deserted barn feels totally dirty and animalistic.

Don't miss out on the opportunity for some food fun, too. Take a picnic with lots of finger foods that you can feed or eat off each other, making the most of the picnic rug or picnic tables when you're alone.

Who doesn't *fancy* a *roll* in the *hay?*

People almost half expect to see shady goings-on in an alleyway, so your actions shouldn't arouse too much interest — unless the local law enforcement happens to be strolling by. Be ready to make a quick getaway if need be.

Alley cats

An alley is dark, dirty and hidden away from the hustle and bustle of the main street, making it perfect for an illicit encounter after dark on the way home. Lean up against the wall for a deep kiss and if this gives you a taste for more, pull her knickers to one side for a quickie.

Sex here taps into any fantasies you may have around prostitution and escorts. A blow job will make you both feel hot and dirty, with him as the client and you the professional. If you like the idea of paying for sex, use language to turn it into a transaction or a power play game.

94

Perfect for illicit encounters

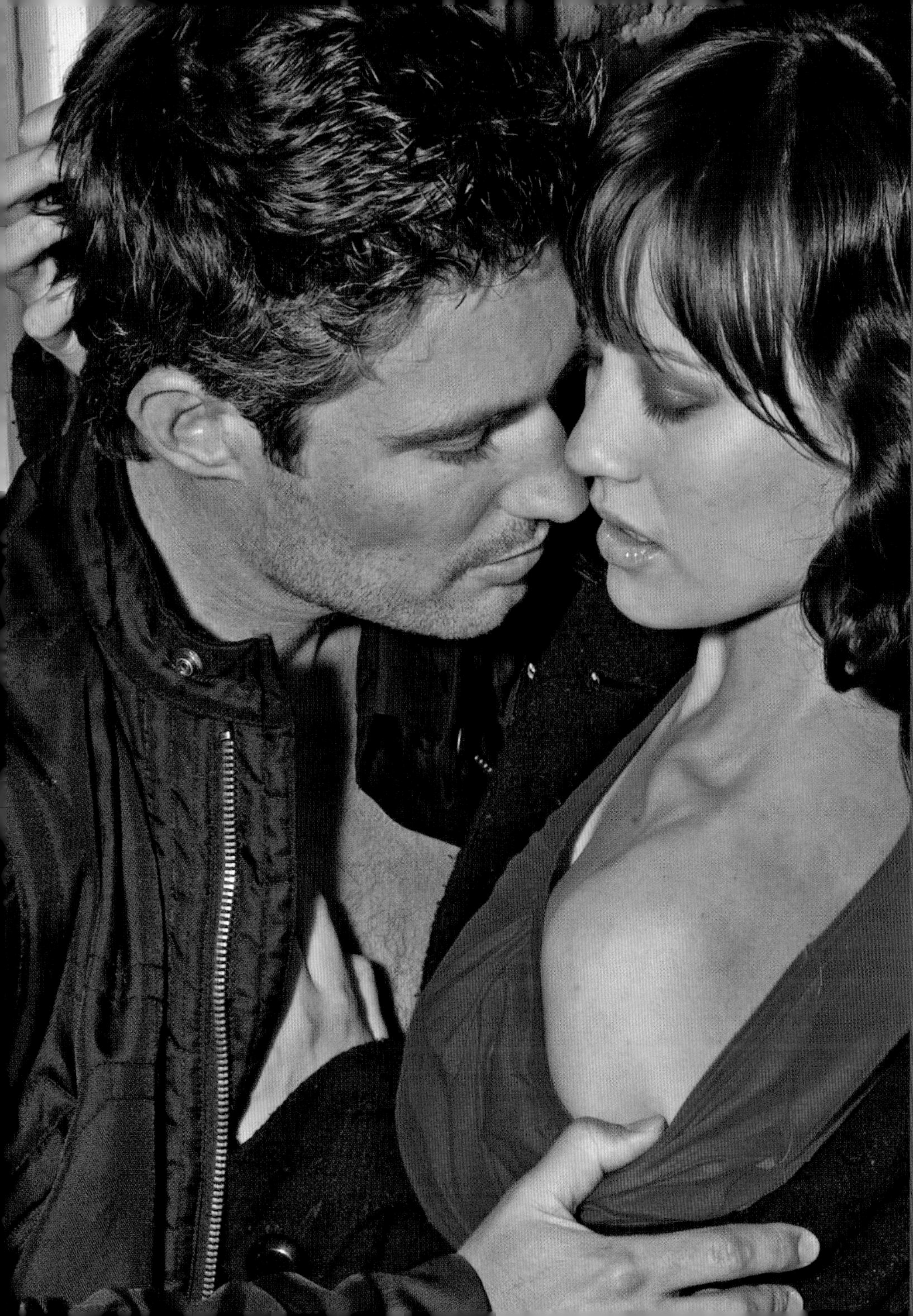

Every woman loves a handyman

Hand jobs are a great way to get to know her body intimately. It's very exciting to see the clitoris become erect. You'll be able to work out what rhythm, pressure and type of movement she needs to orgasm, which you can replicate next time you have sex. The clitoris is highly sensitive and likes to hide beneath its hood so tease it out gently and once she's aroused maintain a steady pace and rhythm to bring her to climax.

Hand jobs for her

Cupping

This technique feels very erotic because you're taking ownership of her vagina. Sit behind her as she nestles between your thighs. Cup her vagina with one hand to build heat. Move the ball of your hand (where it meets the wrist) against her clitoris, keeping your fingers over the entrance of her vagina. Move your hand vertically, horizontally and in concentric circles around her clitoris until she's wet. Then slip two fingers inside (palm up) and stroke her G-spot. She can tense her pelvic muscles to the rhythm of your fingers, which will help her to orgasm.

Riding the wave

This Tantric massage technique is a lovely way to relax and open her vagina. She lies back and you sit to the side of her (use a small cushion in the small of her back to raise her pelvis). Pour lubricant from above so it drips onto her labia, then gently massage her vagina from bottom to top, paying attention to the perineum, outer and inner labia and pubic mound. Squeeze, rub and circle all over to relax her. Do this for a few minutes before massaging her internally. Rub her clitoris with your thumb and penetrate her with your middle finger. Then insert your little finger on the other hand into her anus so that her entire genital area is being massaged. This will lead to a powerful full-body orgasm.

Show him how you like to be touched

Doggy-style

This is a good position for G-spot and deeper vaginal stimulation as the pelvis has free movement. She kneels on all fours while you crouch behind her with one hand between her legs. She can grind into your hand to stimulate her clitoris. Gently roll and pull her clitoris between your thumb and forefinger while you slowly finger her with the other hand. You can also use a small vibrator between her buttocks or to stimulate her internally.

Getting away with it

It's about doing something naughty and taboo, being spontaneous, taking a risk, setting a challenge and expressing a sexual need. Many people find the idea of being watched or caught having sex a turn on.

The exciting rush that accompanies a quickie in public is triggered by a basic physical reaction in the body – the 'flight or fight' response. This normally kicks in when we experience fear, or the fear of getting caught, and it activates adrenaline, noradrenaline and cortisol, which increases heart rate, heightens awareness and causes blood to head to our muscles – so that we can attack or make a quick getaway, or experience an incredible orgasm in minutes! We see and feel things more intensely so having sex at this point feels intoxicating.

Popular locations for fast sex in the public domain include the workplace, on the beach, in a nightclub, on public transport or at a posh do. Next time the urge strikes when you're out and about, give your lover a suggestive look and lead him by the hand to a quiet corner...

100

Sex in public is a common fantasy

Public toilets offer a degree of privacy for both solo and partnered sex antics, with the added frisson of just a door between you and prying eyes. The best cubicles have a full-length door so you can't be seen or heard from outside. Carry a small, quiet vibrator in your bag, a fingertip one will be perfect. Bring yourself to a climax, then re-emerge refreshed and raring to go.

For fun together, plan a special outing and head for the washrooms at a posh hotel – luxurious and relatively quiet (but watch out for washroom attendants!). Dress smartly (a long coat with next to nothing underneath is perfect for getting in the mood) and go into the ladies separately. Although cubicles aren't designed for two,

At your convenience

there are plenty of positions that make for great sex in tight spaces. Try bending over, gripping the back wall with him behind, or stand against the wall with your leg on the seat and him in front. Giving each other some oral pleasure will go down a treat.

A welcome relief
in more ways than one

Pushing the right buttons

Pushing buttons To the next level

104

To the next level

Sex in the lift is exciting and risky. Going all the way may not be possible or practical, but smouldering glances, stolen kisses and hidden caresses, especially in a packed lift, will do for starters (you can always make a swift exit and head for the boardroom...).

Press the 'stop' button between floors for some uninterrupted play. If there's a camera, stand beneath it so it only has a partial view. Keep your moans low key in case there's an audio recording. Release the stop button when you've finished and don't worry about setting the alarm off, you've no idea what happened; the lift just got stuck...

This is an ideal place for a fantasy scenario. Find a quiet lift (or a service elevator), wear loose clothing and no knickers, meet on different floors (perfect for 'stranger' sex play), and go for it. She'll love it if you give her oral sex beneath her coat and if you're in a hotel you can finish off in your room afterwards.

Sometimes the adrenaline and physicality of large crowds can get your pulses racing, and illicit encounters are more thrilling than ever when surrounded by so many bodies. Try a furtive touch beneath big coats in the stands at a sports event.

Rhythmic beats and grinding dance moves are a huge turn on and the atmosphere in a club or at a gig is often charged with sexual tension. In some clubs a quickie in public won't raise any eyebrows, although you may well accrue a few friendly onlookers. Explore your fantasies in public and discover new things that turn you both on.

If you fancy a party with a difference, head to an 'erotic ball' where the bohemian atmosphere is geared towards sexual encounters – flirting, kissing different partners, telling a stranger about your fantasies, watching other people enjoy themselves and exploring your fantasies before finding yourselves a quiet spot to enjoy each other.

Crowd pleasers
Getting caught up in the action

Learning how to have sex standing up is a great skill for exploring outdoor sex. It can be tricky, though, if one of you is much taller than the other and the depth of penetration is limited. Still, it's novel and fun and makes for unforgettable encounters. If there is a height difference try using the stairs, or the woman can wear heels, as this will raise and tighten her buttocks and make penetration snug. Find a door or wall to lean against for support.

Take a stand
When there's standing room only

Three footprints

This fun position allows for plenty of kissing and eye contact to warm you up first. You lean against a wall or tree and he stands in front of you. Once he's inside you, you can wrap your arms around his neck and wind one of your legs around the back of his thigh to pull him in as well as steady yourself. Moving your leg a little higher opens up your vagina and allows him great access for slightly deeper penetration.

Sex in the shower

For shower sex it's best if you are facing the wall with your hands against the tiles for support. Use a non-slip mat to avoid accidents. He wraps his arms around you, cupping your breasts and enters you from behind. Again, the height difference may make this a little tricky so be prepared to bend and squat. He can use his hands to play with your breasts or clitoris once he's inside. If the shower is big enough you can take him deeper by leaning forwards and touching the floor with your hands (those yoga classes are useful for something!). This position is great for G-spot stimulation and will shorten the vaginal passage so that he fits perfectly inside you.

Strong man

This is an energetic position that requires strength and suppleness, so keep it to a quickie and only attempt it if you are much lighter than he is! Start off in the basic standing position where he enters you from the front. Once he's inside you he bends down a little so that you can wrap your legs around his waist and cross them behind his back. This gives you a better range of movement and you can roll your hips and stimulate your clitoris. There's full body contact and he can hold and squeeze your buttocks while he thrusts.

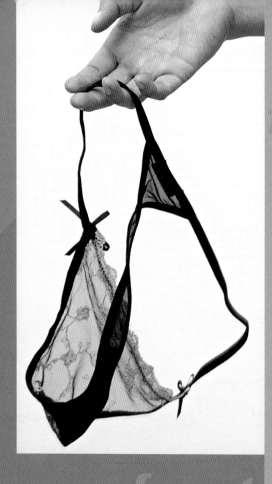

Have you ever found yourself feeling frisky while on a shopping trip? Grab such opportunities for a bit of fun in the seclusion of the changing rooms.

A bra fitting in the lingerie department is perfect – another woman's business-like touch can feel quite erotic and you can see your body and breasts in the mirror. Cupping your breasts to rearrange the bra can lead your thoughts astray and next thing you know there's a tingle between your thighs and you're imagining a different scenario entirely.

A perfect fit

While the assistant goes off to find a few more styles you can watch yourself in the mirror and sit or bend over the stool to play. There's time for a little mischief – send your lover a saucy picture text or video to ask him which style you should go for. Some lingerie shops have peepholes in the door so he can watch you get undressed – the ultimate tease.

The *pleasure*
of a quick change

Who says *working late is a bore?*

There's plenty of fun to be had at work, and a little overtime will pay dividends if you've been working up to it with dirty emails and sexy texts. But be careful – you never know who's monitoring email usage.

Unfinished business

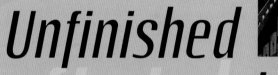

You're halfway to heaven with an office fling and you've probably discovered the delights of flirty looks as well as the strength of your desks. But if your partner or current love interest works elsewhere, you may have to be a little more inventive in sharing a quickie at the office. Arrange for a 'special delivery' to his desk if he's working late and tell the security guys it must be signed for personally.

Keep the heat on when you're apart with sexy underwear beneath your business suit – try stockings and suspenders and a body necklace. If you need to succumb to the 3pm peak in your sex drive, slip off to the toilets with a mini-vibrator in your bag. A post-lunch orgasm will put you in a positive frame of mind for the rest of the day and you can always call your lover to fill him in with the details.

238

Enjoying the
rush hour

Ticket
to ride

With one eye out for CCTV cameras, you can still enjoy the thrill of an illicit rendezvous when commuting. Try a deserted carriage or the top of the bus for a ride to remember, using your coats to disguise wandering hands and hanging on to overhead straps for support. On a packed train, stand behind your lover so she can feel you pressing against her, slipping your hands beneath her top for a nipple massage.

Remote-control sex toys will relieve the boredom of a long journey, especially if he has the controls, or if you're on your own listen to sexy stories on your MP3 player, you'll be fired up by the time you get home.

Joining the Mile High club is a popular fantasy and quickies on a plane are challenging but not impossible. Go separately to the loo, standing behind one another like strangers. Once inside use the toilet seat or sink for support – the vibrations of the cock pit will intensify the experience. Other opportunities might arise, so keep blankets handy for covering laps and wear loose clothing for easy access.

115

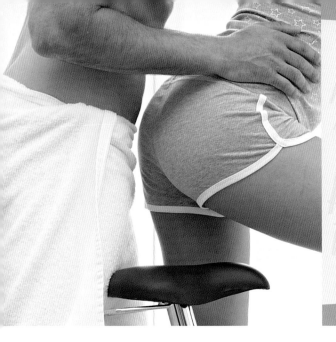

Adding *the* 'personal' *to* personal trainer

Working up a sweat

Exercise is a great precursor to good sex. A workout will get your heart pumping, adrenaline racing and sweat flowing and, what's more, that's a very sexy look for your lover as she won't be able to resist the pheromones you give off.

Once you're hot and sweaty, join each other in the jacuzzi where busy hands will be invisible under the water and you can make use of the jet stream for a little clitoral or cock massage. The sultry atmosphere of the sauna or steam room will soon have you breathing deeply – give him a hand job as he relaxes.

Being semi-naked in public is a turn on in itself, and heading for the pool is a great chance to play in the water with only a scrap of fabric between you. Go when it's quiet and you can try variations on breast stroke and front crawl ... Then head for the unisex changing rooms for a post-shower quickie to relieve all that tension.

Sitting positions are fun and flexible. They're ideal for shallow
penetration if he's not fully erect and work well in cramped spaces. It's
easier if the woman is on top as she can set the pace and position her
pelvis for maximum stimulation. Rocking back and forth together will
increase blood flow and strengthen his erection. To increase resistance
and sensation, move your pelvis away from his and then quickly come
back together again.

Sitting pretty

Yab yum

This is an intimate position in which you can synchronize your bodies and your breathing. He sits upright with his legs crossed and you sit in his lap with your legs wrapped around his back. Put your left hand on the back of his neck and your right at the base of his spine. Once he's inside you, rock back and forth sustaining genital contact. Stroke your right hand up his back to meet the other one. If you lean backwards, he will be able to penetrate you more deeply. When you've finished, come together for a lingering hug and kiss.

Rodeo rider

This technique is good for anonymous sex and G-spot stimulation as you're on top and can move freely. He sits on the edge of the bed and you sit in his lap facing away from him. Guide him inside and then bring your legs together, crossing your ankles to grip him tightly inside. Move your feet against the floor as you rock so that you can push into him vigorously. He should keep his thrusts solid and regular. If you lean forwards and put your hands on the floor, it will lengthen the vaginal canal so you can take him even more deeply.

Spread eagle

This is a variation on the previous technique and allows for either shallow or deep penetration. You sit on the edge of the armchair and he kneels or squats in front of you (use cushions under his knees to make it more comfortable). He enters you holding on to your hips for support. You both rock together with him setting the pace of the thrust. Now pull him forwards while he's still inside you and spread your legs over the sides of the armchair. This move will open up the vagina so that he can thrust quickly and deeply. Choose a firm chair for better support.

Table for two

Ordering off menu

Table for two

A restaurant is a classic venue for seduction; the low lighting, intimate atmosphere and tempting food are irresistible. Dress to impress, making sure that you can reveal a little flesh and sexy lingerie to tantalize in the candlelight.

A secluded alcove and a long tablecloth could lead to plenty of games – slip off your shoes and play footsie under the table, rubbing his penis between your feet, or take it in turns to reveal a body part with each course. A dropped napkin is the perfect excuse to briefly massage your partner's penis as you bend to retrieve it. Feed each other – licking your fingers and lips with a suggestion of things to come.

Once the dessert arrives you'll be primed and ready. Pay the bill and head to the toilets for a quickie or try the lift, an alleyway, the top of the bus or the back of a cab – it'll be difficult to keep your hands off each other until you get home.

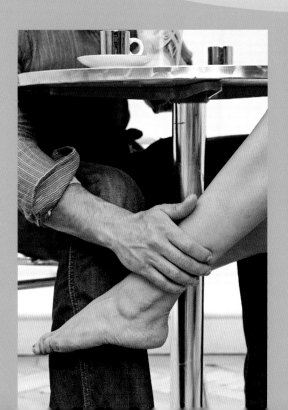

Screen kisses

Put a grown-up twist on teenage fumbles in the cinema – it's dark, warm and intimate, and ideal for a quickie. Select the feature carefully – the latest blockbuster will attract noisy teenagers, more interested in each other than what's going on in the row behind them, and morning or lunchtime screenings will be practically empty.

Choose higher balcony seats if it's an old-fashioned theatre, with no one in front or behind. Drape your coats across your laps and let your hands wander, finding their way through loose clothing.

Don't forget your tub of ice cream for a sensual quickie – try sharing a mouthful in a cool kiss or let it drip down her cleavage then slide your tongue between her breasts to lick it off. A cold tongue running along the shaft of a hot cock will make him shudder with pleasure, or is he getting all emotional at the chick flick on the screen?

Making out on the back row

Ten foolproof excuses

for getting caught
with your pants down ...

1 *'Thanks for your help. I'd have never found my keys without you.'*

2 *'Amazing. I've never seen a [insert wildlife] here before.'*

3 *'Are you sure your car is parked here?'*

4 *'It's only sprained but if you could just help me up I'd be grateful.'*

5 *'Are you sure there's enough light for you to sew the buttons back on?'*

6 *'That last half a mile was a killer. Same time next week?'*

7 *'Is it press-ups, squats or star jumps now? I can never remember the order.'*

8 *'Hello officer, I was just showing her how to change the gears ...'*

9 *'I'm just fixing the photocopier.'*

10 *'Well, she did say the best cure for a headache is sex!'*

the best cure for a headache

'Thanks for 125
your help...
I'd have never
found my keys
without you.'

Index

Acknowledgements

All photographs John Davis/Octopus Publishing, with the exception of the following:

Alamy Nordicphotos/Katrina Dickson 125, Peter Widmann 89

Corbis 81A Productions 92, Anthony Redpath 64, Cathrine Wessel 83, Heide Benser/Zefa 103, Matthew Alan 114, Roy Morsch 90, Simon D Warren/Zefa 33, Tina Chang/Solus-Veer 112

Getty Image Britt Erlanson 19, Christa Renee 79, Christopher Robbins 120, Hummer 113, Maren Caruso 102, Mark Douet 6, Stefano Oppo 88

Jupiterimages 76, Amy Deskin 48, Bananastock 42

Photolibrary Santa Clara/Photononstop 34

Retna UK Ken Bank 105

Executive Editor Jane McIntosh

Senior Editor Charlotte Macey

Executive Art Editor Mark Stevens

Designers Annika Skoog, Rebecca Johns and Paul Reid for Cobalt id

Senior Production Controller Amanda Mackie

Picture Researcher Sally Claxton